TEACHING PHOTOGRAPHY

I0419489

TEACHING PHOTOGRAPHY

NOTES ASSEMBLED
SECOND EDITION

PHILIP PERKIS

Œpress

RIT Cary Graphic Arts Press

2005

Philip Perkis, November, 1935 –
Teaching Photography, Notes Assembled
Teaching, photography and all matters for life

First edition published and designed in 2001 by Œpress, Rochester, NY

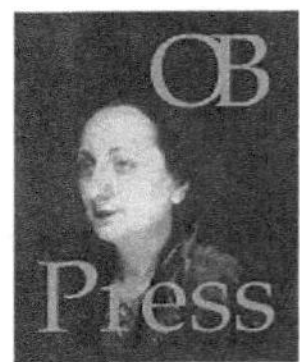
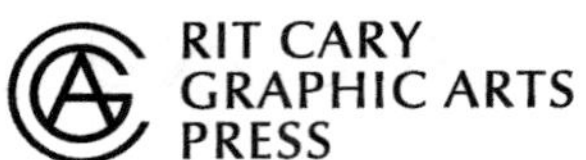

Second Edition
© 2005 Œpress and RIT Cary Graphic Arts Press
All rights reserved.
No part of this book may be used or reproduced in any manner without
written permission, except in the case of brief quotations embodied in
critical articles and reviews.

Distributed by
RIT Cary Graphic Arts Press
90 Lomb Memorial Drive
Rochester, NY 14623
http://wally.rit.edu/cary/carypress.html

ISBN 0-9759651-1-5
Printed in the U.S.A.

'To-find-out-and-elucidate-the-truth-only-through-the-
tonalities-existing-between-white-and-black'
G.I. Gurdjieff ALL AND EVERYTHING

This writing is dedicated to Cyrilla Mozenter, who made it possible.

Edited by Deborah Hussey

Thanks to Owen Butler at Œpress and Zola Logan

CONTENTS

They came in boats and were frightened and sick. They knew they could never go back. They taught their children fear. It was the color of life.

INTRODUCTION

I have taught photography for nearly four decades. Having given countless lectures, assignments and critiques, I felt a need to write down some of my thoughts about the practice of photography and teaching in order to have a sense of completion. These writings have come together in the form of a small book.

Teaching photography, unlike teaching French or driving, provides no sure, measurable result. (How much have I helped a particular person be more sensitive to their visual world?) This puts all of us who teach photography close to the end of the plank – keeping things alive.

The following is not so much to present defensible argument or complete explanations of concepts or technologies. It is rather to set a table that may provoke thought and trigger discussion. Most importantly, to encourage younger photographers and teachers to take some chances.

Go to a museum. Find a photograph that interests you. Look at it for five minutes. Don't take your eye off the picture.

HOW TO TAKE A PICTURE

The object-ness of what is seen. No fast jump to metaphor or symbol. No 'cultural context.' Too soon. Plenty of time for that later. First, the 'reality' of light on surface.

No ideas but in things William Carlos Williams

I have to stay with THAT 'till it's done, and everything I have been taught my whole life is against doing that.

To simply see what something(s) looks like: the light, the space, the relationship (visual) between the distances, the air, the tones, the rhythms, the texture, the contrasts, the shape of movement… the things themselves … not what they might mean later, not socially, not politically, not psychologically, not sexually (a cigar is not even yet a cigar).

Not to name, label, evaluate, like, hate; no memory or desire. Just to see.

This is the hardest thing to do, but that's all that can be photographed. The camera records the light emitted from the surface of that which is placed within its field of view. P e r i o d.

To experience the meaning of what is. To stay with it for even a few seconds is no small task. The sound of voice without language, a musical line, a ceramic vessel, a non-objective painting. The presence of it, the weight of it, the miracle of its existence, of my existence. The mystery of the fact itself.

Maybe it's the second law of infinity where you keep going halfway there forever. Cutting in half to eternity, and 'grace' is needed to jump the gap.

I keep taking pictures hoping something will help me across.

How long does it take to get an Idea?

A photograph is an Idea.

A photograph is an idea manifested outside of time. It is an insight made visible.

The intelligence is pre-logical. This is why it is not possible to separate form and content in a successful photograph; they occur simultaneously. There is, in fact, no difference between them.

There is a photograph by Helen Levitt that shows a group of children playing. One little girl's back is to the camera and a boy is lifting her skirt and 'peeking.'

The photograph is at once funny, sad and frightening. I think it's a masterpiece. This picture could only be a photograph. This kind of metaphor, this poignant taste, comes from the unique directness of the medium.

The kind of emotional resonance that photography evokes is more akin to what can happen in poetry and music rather than to visual disciplines such as painting, drawing and sculpture.

> *I set out now*
> *in a box*
> *upon the sea.*
> Charles Olson *Maximus Poems*

I don't think it's arbitrary that Jack Kerouac refers to Robert Frank's book, *The Americans*, as a blues.

Photography and writing always refer to something outside of each medium. There is always description of some sort. It's true that over the years people have tried to fight this in both. The pictorialist photographers of the late-19th century tried to make photographs look like paintings and lithographs. This work is generally thought of as being rather silly now.

There is, of course, a return to this genre with a contemporary group of 'art saucers,' who are trying to convince people that a lack of information in a picture constitutes a mystery. 'Bet you can't guess what this is a picture of?' Why is this interesting?

Many writers such as James Joyce, William Carlos Williams and
William Burroughs, have tried breaking the form in their attempts
to get away from a traditional narrative in order to embrace a larger
emotional and intellectual landscape. They are less interested in
'factual truth' than emotional truth. This is not the same as with-
holding information in order to create something for the appear-
ance of mystery.

> *There is nothing more mysterious than a fact clearly stated.*
> Garry Winogrand (probably stolen from Francis Bacon)

Painting, music, sculpture and drawing do not have to refer to
anything outside of the work itself. They can, but they don't have to.

I don't believe that Agnes Martin or Mark Rothko would want
us to think of their paintings as being about anything (as subject
matter) other than what's on the surface of the paintings themselves. I am not talking about possible journeys of emotion, spirit,
or even physical sensation that can occur when confronting these
works.

As far as music is concerned, Leonard Bernstein set musical
understanding back about fifty years by encouraging us to look
for content other than in the music itself. In the 'Young People's
Concerts' of the early 1950s, he told children to imagine men on
horses charging when they listened to Beethoven's Fifth Symphony.

This issue is a slippery business. The paradox is that in photography, its ability to describe is at once its strength and uniqueness
as visual expression, and at the same time this very quality makes
it one of the most difficult of forms to master because of its urge to
be literal. I can move in a good direction with this by understanding
that while realism and abstraction appear to work in opposition, a
harmonious relationship can be created between them. To accept
this paradox allows for something profound to occur.

When watching a Balanchine ballet, I am not for a moment thinking that what I am seeing is other than human bodies in space, but
what moves me is the abstract quality of the movement, shapes,
rhythm, color, space, etc. Description and abstraction in harmonious tension.

Another way into this idea is to look at the work of Walker Evans
and consider that he may be one of the great abstract artists of the
20th century, even though he is thought to be primarily a documentary photographer. Look at the prints upside down and the remark-
able architecture of the frame becomes more apparent. Cartier-
Bresson used to edit his contact sheets upside down in order to see
the abstraction first.

Many of us edit first from negatives instead of contact sheets in
order to see shapes, tones and spaces before we see details of subject matter.

Art lives in the tension between
abstraction ⟷ ⟷ ⟷ ⟷ ⟷ description

This is similar to Hans Hoffman's concept of 'push-pull' that he beat
the abstract expressionists over the head with in the 1950s.

The following questions are to be answered as thoughtfully as possible.

What is art?

What is the function of the artist in the world?

Why do you want to engage in art-making?

Why are some activities thought of as 'art' (painting, music) and others not (engineering, sociology)?

What is the difference between 'fine' art and 'commercial' or 'applied' art?

Which living artist do you feel kinship with?

Which dead artist do you feel kinship with?

What is the function of 'talent' in art-making?

What is the relationship between art and the political, economic world?

What is the relationship between art and the religious (spiritual) world?

What is the relationship between art and nature?

PHOTOGRAPHY AS THE CAUSE OF THE DOWNFALL OF WESTERN CIVILIZATION

In his essay *The Human Universe*, Charles Olson postulates that since the Greeks, our system of language has become more and more about description of intellect and concept and has lost its ability to express experience directly.

When Diane Arbus committed suicide in 1971 (that her death was a suicide is relevant because her life then took on a quality of legend), the Museum of Modern Art in New York mounted a large retrospective exhibition of her photographs. It was the most highly attended show in the museum's history. A large percentage of the work concerned itself with photographs of people 'on the fringe.'

She had the ability to photograph ordinary people and create a feeling of alienation and strangeness in the picture. Perhaps we photograph to find reflection of inner emotional qualities (Another way of looking at Stieglitz's concept of equivalence?)

I spent some time hanging around at the show because I never felt that her work was that important or profound as to warrant the attention it was getting. I wanted to find out why this was so.

A lot of the viewers seemed to be conventional sorts, not people of the 'avant-garde,' and certainly few 'outsiders.'

Over many visits, I overheard some variation of, 'Oh, I'm so glad I don't have to meet that person,' several dozen times at least.

I began to understand something. Photography provides a window through which we can see things that we fear or do not want to have contact with directly. It's not just about seeing things that are not available or no longer exist such as Abraham Lincoln or the Hindenberg.

A noteworthy industry of the mid-to-late-19th century was the 'photographic freak show.' Nadar was doing it back in the 1840s with his gender-bending nudes, and later Muybridge, with his 'scientific' studies of naked people doing all kinds of things, not to mention exposed breasts, and bones through noses, as well as dozens of albums of freaks and diseases that were produced as 'scientific' studies. Robert Mapplethorpe and Larry Clark are not new.

The year 1839 then, simply benchmarks the technology that allows for the ability to fix on a surface the lens or monocular vision that had been used in painting, drawing and printmaking for the previous several hundred years. That's when the separation began. If one accepts the idea that the development of 'realism' in art encouraged separation from direct experience in a similar way that the development of Western language to some degree prevents people from the direct expression of sensation, then an idea is starting to develop.

If we start with the phenomenon of realism in painting and then add the pervasive and ubiquitous presence and power of photography, film and video, we can see how they have had an enormous and profound effect on the psyche of people. The direction of this shift has encouraged us to relate to each other in an increasingly less direct manner. It has altered every aspect of our lives – and not always in a positive way. It has allowed and encouraged people to experience many more things vicariously. Most people have never actually seen a person being shot to death, and yet there are over 1,200 deaths by guns shown on television every day.

If I look at painting and drawing before artists began to use the lens as an aid with the camera obscura and camera lucida, it is abundantly clear that the function of visual art was other than to create the illusion of reality. To say that the invention of monocular vision and perspective and its use in artworks is an 'improvement' over less intelligent efforts that preceded it is ridiculous, even possibly chauvinistic.

This is not to suggest that the inventors of this system were guilty of anything. It is what this system has to come to signify in relation to culture and how we define it.

Perhaps it may have something to do with Western Europeans

having seen themselves as being the center or model of what a civilized people should be, everything else being a bit 'primitive' or at least peripheral.

There is nothing original in suggesting that the function of art is in the area of expressing and transmitting a certain quality of knowledge that cannot be expressed using ordinary discourse.

The only possible reason for writing a poem is that what is being spoken of cannot be expressed as well using prose form.

If I sit in a museum and look at a carpet from Central Asia, it is clear that this object is not simply decorative. There are levels of meaning and value that are beyond my rational mind to comprehend. If, however, I sit for awhile and open myself up to just looking without trying to figure out meaning as though it were an arithmetic problem, then something can take place in me that is at once subtle, profound and most importantly, not translatable into language. One can write and speak about the taste of vanilla with the intelligence and eloquence of the best wordsmith; I still don't know the taste of vanilla. But, if I hear and read these descriptions, and then taste vanilla for the first time, I might say, 'of course.' This can be equally true of visiting the Grand Canyon or viewing a work of art for the first time.

The question, of course, remains as to whether the technology drives social, psychological and cultural changes, or does the psyche of the culture create a vacuum, which a technology is created to fill. It seems to me that the question has no definitive answer, but the relationship is fascinating and always worth looking at.

EXERCISE #2 PUSHPINS

Put two pushpins in the wall about six inches apart. Sit 15 feet away and relax for a minute or so. Look at the pushpin on the right. Look hard. Now shift your attention to the pushpin on the left. You will notice the pushpin that you are not paying attention to appears less distinct. A bit out of focus.

EXERCISE #3 HOW TO LOOK

Sit back and relax the muscles of your eyes so that you see the 'field' more completely and your eyes jump from object to object a little less. This requires a purposeful effort, but it helps photographic practice a great deal.

When I was a child, maybe nine or ten, one of the cubbyholes that they pushed learning into was called 'science.' I think they pushed things into these cubbyholes so that young people would never get a sense of the connectedness of things. If they did, they might not sit still long enough to be fed through the system we call 'culture' and become 'productive citizens.'

Anyway, back to this 'science.' The teacher is seldom the person who loves science and runs home after school to the basement to do experiments and research.

The teacher explains that the human eye is just like a camera; light goes through the lens, stimulates the rods and cones and sends signals up the optic nerve to the brain, which then interprets what is seen. It's a one-way street.

There are even charts and diagrams to make it more understand-
able. It's really neat, except it's not true.

If I sit quietly for a moment on a park bench or on a rock in the
forest and start to pay attention to how I see, I begin to realize that
what is happening is that my vision shifts from point to point at an
incredible speed. I focus my attention from object to object. In other
words, I am 'looking around.' My mind is assembling a picture that
I experience as a whole. So something quite different from that silly
chart is going on. Somehow my brain and eyes are in cahoots. It's a
two-way street.

§§§§§

I am walking down the street and see someone interesting on the
other side. I quickly raise my camera and click. The picture reveals
four cars, three buildings, two dogs and 18 people other than the
one who caught my fancy. The camera did what the 'science'
teacher said the eye does.

Is there a way out of this? Maybe. Yes. A few possibilities:

Run across the street and get close to the subject. The problem
here is that when I get there it's too late or the other person has
seen me and the picture is then a portrait – or they get angry and
turn away. This method, as well as the telescopic lens solution, also
eliminates the context in which the subject exists, which is what
probably attracted me in the first place.

It is not possible for anyone to create a coherent, intelligent and
possibly emotive photograph from most of what is seen –
meaningful or not.

Yogi Berra was in a slump. The coach told him to think about
what he was doing when batting. He got up to the plate and struck
out. Returning to the dugout, he said, 'You can't bat and think at
the same time.'

When I photograph, I am trying to grasp the 'whole.' This requires
me to trust my instinct and impulse of the moment. I cannot do it
with thinking alone.

It helps to use the same lens all the time because one gets used to
the field of vision of that lens and can grasp the whole more quickly.

Zoom lenses are the work of the devil. They are seldom sharp on
the edges, and more importantly they don't encourage a person to
establish a real 'point of view.'

The genius of Eugene Atget is that he always knew exactly where
to place the camera. This is a perfect blending of the physical,
aesthetic and philosophical aspects of art-making.

> *Position is where everything happens from.*
> Frederick Sommer

It helps to realize that the frame is not a natural thing at all, it is an
imposition on vision. The paradox, of course, is that the frame is
a very important contributor to content in a photograph. What is
included, what is left out, and what is cut can be, and frequently is,
the central meaning in a photograph.

When my daughter Rachel was about two years old, she became obsessed with elephants. There were some elephant books with pictures and a record with an elephant song. This went on for several weeks, which is a long time for a small child.

Saturday came and I took her to the Central Park Zoo to see the real thing. She was beside herself with excitement. This was before the 'improvement' of the zoo and the elephant house was cement – dark, humid and odorous.

I took her on my shoulders (our favorite way to travel in the city) and I pointed to the elephant who was about 15 feet away. She couldn't see it.

I backed up as far as space permitted, maybe 40 feet. She still could not see it. The elephant was right in front of her and she could not see it. It was too large.

Rachel got quite upset. I was profoundly shaken. We went outside and had ice cream.

§§§§§

Photographs do not show size, only relationships.

Francis Frith was sent from England to photograph Egypt in 1858, he put people, animals and carts into the frame in order to show the size of the objects because the viewers of these pictures had no reference of scale in their experience.

Other examples of this are:
Timothy O'Sullivan's 1873 photograph with a yardstick next to an inscribed rock.

Manuel Alvarez Bravo's sand piles (circa 1920s) with twigs in front of the wall of a house.

More recently, Thomas Demand's models of office interiors photographed with no scale reference.

It's simple to say that photographs don't show absolute size, only relative size, and let it go at that; however, it might be more interesting to think about the idea that nothing is a size in and of itself, only in relation to other things can size be understood.

Rulers, odometers, range finders and a host of other devices (including hands) have been developed and agreed upon as standard ways to reference size. We no longer remember that these devices are simply a useful way to communicate.

An ant crossing the floor can be a wondrous event if I allow myself to just watch.

I went to a small park in Tel Aviv with my friend and his five-year-old daughter. There was a pond with goldfish. The child got quite interested and watched the fish for some time. When we got back to my friend's house, the girl told her mother about seeing the fish. Her mother asked if there were any large ones. 'Oh yes,' the girl said. 'Some were small,' and she held her fingers about one inch apart, 'and some were big,' and she held her fingers about three inches apart.

The practice of photography can help me to again experience some things that, through what we call 'education,' I have outgrown and forgotten.

Go anywhere to photograph in your usual way. For one roll, every time you take a picture, turn around and quickly take a second picture of whatever you see that was in back of you.

§§§§§

Many years ago, the painter Raymond Parker wrote an essay on the idea of intention in art-making. As I remember it, his basic thesis was that without intention there can be no art. Makes sense. If I want to build Chartres Cathedral or make a dramatic film then it is clear that my intention must precede the execution of these projects. At every point of building a structure or making a film, decisions are made both large and small, conscious and unconscious, that significantly affect the result. It still remains that there was a 'plan' needed first and that plan is an expression of intent.

Let's go a different way. I set up an arena where something can take place. Then I see what happens. John Cage did this in music and called it 'Chance Operations.' People who play improvisational music do this all the time. There have been many experiments in theater and performance art that have been based on this idea.

Spalding Gray did a show called *Interviewing the Audience* around 1980. It was a brilliant example of setting a stage and then improvising within the boundaries.

As a photographer, I decide on a certain set of materials (camera, lens, film) and I take myself somewhere at a certain time. It could be my backyard or living room; it doesn't have to be Outer Mongolia. Then I'm going to see what happens. I become an active responder to what is happening both inside and outside of myself. I do my best not to consider content or meaning at this time.

Then, putting myself in that position physically, emotionally and mentally, I can have an 'open' attitude toward what I am doing so that with a bit of luck (grace) my intention can arise simultaneously with the act of photographing.

Alfred Hitchcock said that he never considered content when making a film. He just concentrated on moving the story along.

This attitude is no less intentional than planning ahead. If anything, it can be more intentional because it involves more of me in the activity. In a sense, I'm turning some of the responsibility over to my instinct, impulse and receptivity, and taking a little heat off my mind, which just might let it function better than when it has to carry the whole weight of the job.

It should be pointed out that in photography I don't print everything I shoot. In fact, I print very, very little. This lets me take enormous risks when I photograph. My intention can be re-formed in editing. By emphasizing certain aspects of tone when I print, I can reinforce intention. So, in a way, I have three chances.

I once sat breathless for about 20 minutes at the Brooklyn Academy of Music with about 1,500 other people while Julius Hemple stood alone on stage playing improvisationally on a tenor saxophone. That's high risk art-making. His intentionality was palpable. He had no cover.

From the beginning, photography has occupied a maverick position in relation to the art world. Many of the greatest pictures have been made by professional photographers on assignment. The intent of the assigners was not that transformative images would be created. Just a few examples to make this clear: the work of Timothy O'Sullivan, Dorothea Lange and Walker Evans. These examples are easy; with a little stretch, one can even see a 'magic' quality in some of the photographs that Charles Sheeler made of art objects for the Metropolitan Museum while working on staff. It seems possible that if a photographer simply observes something with enough receptivity and intelligence, and then applies impeccable craft in the recording of that subject, that something in the realm of what we think of as 'art' can emerge.

Since photographs don't have the physical presence of most paintings and sculptures (surface, texture, evidence of gesture, size, etc.), then the imprint of the photographer's vision is not as easily discernible as, say, in the paintings of Giorgio Morandi or William Bailey. This keeps photography an unpredictable and surprising medium in that the traditional terms used to discuss the visual arts do not necessarily apply. Photographs can be no more than a direct bridge between the subject and the viewer. The viewer can be either the photographer or the person looking at the photograph or both. And how the photographer got there is indescribable and mysterious. It stops dead in their tracks, those who would explain the whole business for us and make logical and predictable the content of photographs.

I can stand in a certain place – I can never be quite sure of how to get into that position – and look at something in front of me – I can never be sure of what that subject should be – put a small box that records light coming from that object between me and it, and the result can be transcendent and emotionally charged. I don't know exactly how that happens and I hope I never will.

§§§§§

Because of its renegade nature, photography as an 'art' medium has supported some of the silliest, lightweight stuff imaginable, all the way from Henry Peach Robinson on. Pictures that would probably not be taken seriously in other mediums are given weight in the photographic world. Indeed, such pictures can be seen in museums and scholarly articles have been written about them. In the end, I think this is a small price to pay for the freedom from the Academy that photography has enjoyed.

Sometime in the 1970s, photographs started to been seen as commodity. Before that, they were seen more as evidence of the photographer's vision or concept, and the print itself had little physical or monetary value. As time went by photographs were beginning to be worth real money, particularly if the photographer was dead or the print was large or there was an 'idea' in the picture that could be written about. There were articles being written about the possibility that photography was 'Art.' People even took sides. To this day, the dance continues.

Several years ago I met a photographer named Hector Garcia. It was in Guadalajara at one of those gatherings of photographic types called a symposium.

Hector was no longer young and not always sober, but he had a great spirit and a wonderful tale to tell.

He spoke of being very young, a child, living in the extreme poverty of Mexico City. When his mother went to work, out of desperation she would tie him to the bed in a dark room.

There was a keyhole in the door that quite by accident functioned as a pin-hole lens and projected the activities of the street onto the wall opposite. That became Hector's world of impressions. He said it was this experience (he did not say how long it lasted) that was his first photography. He has continued for the next 70 or so years to make pictures.

At the final meeting of the symposium, Hector took off all his clothes backstage hoping that some of the women photographers would take pictures of him. I'm not sure of the connection between the two events, but the bittersweet quality of both is quite telling.

His tale also seems to demonstrate that photographic imagery is not an invention at all, but rather a phenomenon that occurs when circumstances converge in a certain way, similar to rainbows and hail.

Is it possible that this is why some of the animals in cave paintings of pre-history are upside down? Photographic projection does that.

Because of its directness, immediacy and narrative possibility, the medium of television is immeasurably powerful and influential. It forms 'reality' for much of our contemporary culture.

§§§§§

Some years back I did a small assignment using Kodachrome film, which at the time was the most detailed, saturated color film available. When I got the slides from the lab, I needed a place to project them.

On a whim, I taped a piece of white paper to the front of the television set and used that as a screen. After looking at the slides and editing them, I took down the paper. Later that day, I turned on the television. I had a strange feeling. I put the white paper back and projected the slides again. Then, I watched television again.

§§§§§

Television is not as much of a visual medium as we assume, because everything looks pretty much the same on it. I think that television is more of a literary, narrative medium. If you look carefully at a video image, you can see that there is very little visual subtlety in that the actual tone and color are rather crude compared to other visual media.

This is beginning to change with high-definition video, but there are about three generations that think they were raised in a visual world and, in fact, they were not.

Why can't Johnny see?

When a very small child sees the dog, points and says, 'dog,' the parents go nuts with enthusiasm and think the kid is a genius.

The message is clear; in our culture the purpose of vision is to name and to classify. That's where the 'money' is.

What about the way light describes the dog's fur in the sun, in the shade; at night, with ghostlike moves in the hall? What of the shape of movement of the tail when happy or frightened, the tilt of the head, the messages that can be received through tiny body gestures that cannot be verbalized? How about the way the dog animates a room with its movements. And on and on. No rewards for any of this. The naming is what counts. Intelligence is measured in reading and math scores. When was the last scholarship given to someone for being receptive and observant?

How about a school system where the children spend six hours a day on art, poetry, music, dance, photography, painting, and so on. Twice a week the English teacher comes in with a cart to teach spelling and grammar for 40 minutes. The math teacher would do the same on alternate days. Then when there is a budget squeeze, people plead and have bake sales to save the English program because the art program is unassailable.

The illiterate of tomorrow will be the person
who doesn't understand photography.
Edward Steichen (probably stolen from Man Ray)

Expose a whole roll of film on one subject; a person, place, thing, group of things.

§§§§§

It is commonplace to think that photographing involves finding something interesting, taking a picture of it, putting away the camera until something else interesting is noticed, taking a picture of that, and so on. This may not be the most profound use of the medium.

There is a photograph by Andre Kertész of a fork resting on the edge of a plate. The fork casts a shadow. That's all there is. The picture is transformative. There are hundreds of examples of this in the history of art. Who cares about the apples in Cezanne's pictures or even the particulars of Van Gogh's postman. In art, it's not so much the object depicted, but rather what happens when it is transformed through a medium by a particular artist's sensibility. This is not such an easy thing to learn in photography because the medium encourages literalness by its very nature.

If and when I get a sense of why a simple Korean ceramic vessel, or the sound of Lester Young playing the melody of a popular song on a scratched record, can be among the highest forms of human expression, then I am beginning to discover what 'art' is. I certainly cannot do this with my rational mind alone. Something else in me is beginning to function at these moments.

CONTRAST AND VALUE IN
BLACK & WHITE & COLOR

In black and white photography the contrast (lightness next to darkness) is created by the amount or percentage of light reflected from any given area as seen from the point of view of the lens. A dark object reflects less of the light falling on it than a light one. Modern black and white films are panchromatic. That is to say, they record all colors with equal value. Yellow, red and other colored filters placed in front of the lens can be used to change these relationships (a yellow filter will make blue darker, etc.) This is not a good idea for new photographers because it does not encourage the development of the ability to observe subtle values, and this is crucial.

When photographing in black and white, we are continually engaged in a process of translation. This becomes intuitive after a time. In other words, the yellow shirt and pink pants against the blue wall photographed with color film would have great contrast, but in black and white it is possible (if they all have the same value) that the photograph could be very flat and gray.

Color photographs provide the viewer more information. It's not a light or dark car, it's a green light or dark car.

This may sound a bit simple-minded until we begin to consider the visual, psychological, and even political possibilities in this translation or non-translation.

A black and white photograph of a Chinatown gift shop would be a greater descriptive departure than a black and white photograph of most modern office furniture showrooms.

The elements that create the sense of abstraction in color are very different than the elements that hold that function in black and white because color is more descriptive and informational.

Find a room where sun comes in late in the day. Place a comfortable chair that looks toward the light and sit down. Sit there until it's dark. Just watch.

§§§§§

When I was a student at the San Francisco Art Institute, we had a senior seminar class with Fred Martin. It took place in a large room with a skylight. There were people who worked in every medium and we would discuss our work. We met from four to seven in the afternoon and Fred Martin would not let us turn on the lights. Everything changed with the light during those three hours: the work, the people, the space, the tone of voice, our relationships with one another – everything. It was revelatory.

Thank you, Fred Martin.

THE ZONE SYSTEM

In the fall of 1958, I began to study photography at the California
School of Fine Arts. Later the name changed to the San Francisco
Art Institute. One of the classes required of all photography stu-
dents (there were about 10 of us) was with Ansel Adams.

At one of the first meetings, he took us out to the backyard of the
school with a Polaroid camera, which at the time was a rare item.
Ansel had some sort of arrangement with the company so he got
a lot of their materials and they got some of his pictures to use in
advertising promotion.

There was a door. With the aid of his S.E.I. meter, Ansel was
going to render the door zone V. He said that he would then render
it zone II and then zone VIII. It didn't work out. Polaroid prints
and all the debris that they leave behind started to accumulate over
the yard. When he said he was doing zone V he would get zone III
or VII, etc. A lot of film was used. Ansel was getting more and more
upset and we started to giggle. That was my introduction to the
zone system. A few weeks later Ansel stopped teaching at the school
saying that he was too busy. He said he didn't think we were very
serious students anyway.

If I sit in a room and look around when the light is not particularly
dramatic, I will be hard-pressed to identify any object or part of an
object that is an untextured black. If I then shift my attention to the
other side of the tonal scale, I will also be hard-pressed to identify
any object that is an untextured white.

There are very few instances of black or white in our visual
lives. If I go out at night in the city, I will see almost no untextured
black, but some white because of light sources. Consequently, if I
want to make a photograph that renders the tones of the subject
and gives the illusion of faithfulness – I use the term faithfulness
rather than 'realistic' or 'accurate' because these terms do not

apply to photographs, the print will rarely contain untextured black or white. It's important to point out that this is not a moral issue or even an aesthetic one; it is a way to understand the process and how to use it. Many important photographs have been made using paper white and untextured black.

If I then choose to introduce areas of black or white in my prints it will be with intention rather than neglect. Clearly, when the exposure is made, enough light must be allowed to strike the film so that the darkest objects are affected to some degree. Therefore, exposure is determined by the darkest significant area of the picture. If an area gets no exposure, then even if the film is developed for a week, there will be no image and the print will be black in that area.

The degree of development is determined by four factors: Strength of developer, Temperature of developer, Agitation given, Length of time of the development. The more the film is developed, the more density the lighter areas of the picture will contain. Therefore, these areas will tend to be lighter in the print.

That is the principle; how it's used depends on how one wants to work. The view-camera person can measure and test to a point where everything is completely predictable. (Minor White's *Zone System Manual* will get you there without much pain.)

The small-camera user can simply pay attention to the shadows and find a developing time and temperature that will generally place tones in a way that the desired contrast can be arrived at with the use of filters when printing. (This is explained by David Vestal in *The Art of Enlarging*.)

Technology is not the central issue. The problem lies in the growth of a sensitivity on the part of the photographer toward the use of tone as content in making pictures that have real substance. *M*usical tone, tone of *v*oice, emotional tone, tone *p*oem, tone *v*ibrations, tone of *m*ovement.

EXERCISE #7 PHOTOGRAPHING LIGHT

Expose a roll or two of film so that if someone viewing the
resulting prints were to be asked, 'what is the subject?' they
would reply, 'light.'

My aim, as I said in the introduction, isn't to write yet another book on how to develop film. At the same time, I've chosen to include some technical information that might be helpful. Experience has shown me that if I figure out and follow up the development of film in a very controlled way, I can be quite loose in choosing my exposures when I take pictures, and be more present to what is going on in front of me.

Film development is the main determining factor of contrast in a photograph after, of course, the actual contrast of the subject. Through film development I can have the tonal relationships of most negatives placed in such a way that I have great latitude of choice when I print – except in extreme situations like black cats in the snow on sunny days or gray cats on the beach in heavy fog. Printing then becomes interpretive rather than remedial.

> *The negative is the score and the print, the performance.*
> Ansel Adams

Just a few particulars:

Metal tanks and reels are preferable to plastic ones because the metal reels are open, allowing the chemicals to flow more evenly across the film surface. Metal will not hold chemical traces and can be washed more thoroughly than plastic, which to some degree is absorbent. The down side of metal reels is if you drop one, it bends and it's dead. My preference is for the four-reel metal tanks because if I use larger ones, agitation becomes erratic.

A consistent thermometer is crucial. It need not be correct as long as it's consistent. Protect it from physical shocks and don't lend it out. Use a timer that starts and stops.

Try to have the temperature of the room be close to the temperature of the developer or use a large tray of room-temperature water to stand the tank in. Don't hold the tank in your hands while developing, it will heat up.

Establish an absolute system for pouring in and pouring out the developer as well as a consistent agitation pattern. It doesn't matter what it is as long as it's the same every time.

The developer temperature should be within one half degree of your intention. The rest of the chemicals can be within three or four degrees.

If I develop film in a different water system, the pH of the water may be different and will affect the degree of development. (I guess one could use distilled water. I don't.)

The longer that film is wet, the more the emulsion will swell, causing the grain to soften and enlarge, making the print a little mushy. I like to use a developing time of less than 10 minutes, one minute water bath (to build the shadows a little more), a rapid fix and a wash aid that keeps the wet time down to about 20 minutes. If the developing time is less than five minutes, it's hard to be exact enough.

I don't sponge or squeegee film after Photoflo – on several occasions a bit of grit was picked up at the top of the roll, scratching the whole length. I would rather let the film dry a little longer.

I use a set of four tanks lined up in the sink and start developing at one minute intervals, which is maintained through the whole process, so that I can develop 16 rolls of film in under an hour.

Ever since the power people decided that photography is an Art, just as in creating God in man's image rather than the other way around, a lot of people are trying to make photographs that look like Art rather than enlarging the concept of what art is or what it should look like.

Prints are getting bigger while ideas are getting smaller. If one looks carefully at most of the very large prints in galleries and museums, it is clear that most of the pictures are not very interesting if you take away the size factor. Remember the ant? By trying to make photographs more than what they inherently are, we LOSE what they inherently are, and the magic disappears.

Since photographs are not very complex physically, the difference between an ordinary picture of something and a photograph that has a transcendent or other emotive quality can be extremely subtle and fragile. I'm not suggesting that making large prints is wrong, it's just not necessarily a gain and can be a loss.

EDITING AND PRINTING
BLACK & WHITE PHOTOGRAPHS

After the bathroom, the most important room in the house is the darkroom.

Over the years, I have met many people who say they love photography, but hate film development and printing. When I ask them about where they work, it's generally some variation of 'in the cellar behind the furnace with a plastic tent on a bridge table, no air and water 40 feet away.' Who would want to do anything in a place like that?

For me printing is a contemplative activity. At best, I don't always try to get much done. Sometimes I go into the darkroom, mix up the chemicals and spend a couple of hours drinking coffee and looking at negatives and contact sheets. Not printing at all. Would you ask a poet, 'How many poems did you write today?'

I have contact sheets and negatives together. There is a small light box near the enlarger and a good loupe. I look at negatives and contacts at the same time. Contact sheets tell me more about subject matter, particularly facial expression. Negatives, on the other hand, tell much more about tone, sharpness, scale and space. I see the formal structure of a picture better from the negative than from the contact print.

By looking at both I get the most information. I simply look. When a negative attracts my attention for any reason, I make a quick print. What I am trying to do is keep the process of editing as close to the act of photographing as possible. My first prints are on resin-coated paper and are always full frame. I make a lot of these fast prints. They become the arena for editing.

If a serious and prolific photographer were to die, and the negatives given to other photographers or editors who had never seen the work, it's safe to suggest that they would be far off the mark in presenting the work of this photographer's intentions. Just consider what was done to Kertész and Winogrand by people who not only knew them, but were even friends.

Editing, then, becomes the place where 'content' is dealt with. The other thing that takes place at this stage is that I begin to consider what a picture does in relation to other pictures. How they speak to each other. A picture placed next to another can alter the 'meaning' and sense of both, sometimes radically.

So I now have a big bunch of proof prints. Maybe one or two are just simply fabulous, and I know it. Good. I pin them all to the wall in a place with good light and over a period of about a week they will almost edit themselves. I will find myself taking the weak ones down, and most importantly, I learn more about how I see the world. Once again the photographs are evidence of experience and this evidence will lead to further experience.

> *One perception must immediately and*
> *directly lead to a further perception.* Edward Dahlberg

I think it axiomatic to state that even the best photographers produce very few truly first-rate pictures in a lifetime.

Several years ago, there were two retrospective Henri Cartier-Bresson exhibitions within a few months of each other. One had about 124 prints and the other about 75. The smaller show was stronger by far, and this from a brilliant photographer who worked constantly for about 60 years with only a little time off to be a prisoner of war.

Even Winogrand, who burned enough film to make Mister Kodak weep for joy, gets weak after about 50 pictures. Perhaps it's the funnel metaphor: no matter how big the top, only a certain amount can come out the bottom.

My purpose here is practical. It divides the editing process into two aspects. The first is the fluid activity of photographing, developing film, and making a lot of fast prints in order to track my progress and learn more and more about photography, my vision, and my relation to what I see and experience as my world.

The second process is to keep a keen eye for when things come together to make a negative that is a benchmark of that process in which I am engaged. What might be for me an important picture.

A balance must be kept between the two processes; if I only deal with the first, I will become inattentive and 'anything will do.' If I over emphasize the second, then I can only take pictures that I have already seen – either my own or someone else's. I am no longer open to the process of discovery, which for me is the *tsimis* of the thing.

At this point, I have a small group of pictures from which I want to make finished prints. This calls for another shift. My attitude at this time is that I am interpreting the picture. I crop the negative at this point by masking on the proof print in different ways. One thing that I try to do in cropping is to take some off both the sides, top and bottom, in order to keep the shape of the format intact. (It's one of my compulsions.)

I have never been successful at cropping a great deal of the picture, although some great photographers are big croppers. Helen Levitt says that it gives you 'a second chance.'

The danger for new photographers in cropping is that it may encourage them to be less rigorous when taking pictures. Photoshop brings up this issue in a huge way. (See chapter on the Digital Revolution.)

The other problem is that one may tend to make pictures that are over-simplified because you can 'clean them up by cropping.'

It seems that there are no rules about cropping pictures except to say that it should be done with care and intelligence. I try not to give up the full frame too easily.

At one point several years ago, I had a sign over the sink in my darkroom that read 'Slow down.' I then spent several hundred

dollars buying a fancy print washer mostly because it would only
hold 12 prints. It's so easy to make a ton of mediocre prints in four
or five hours. It's expensive too.

I put the cleaned negative in the enlarger. (A simple way to get dust
off the negative is to turn off the lights, turn on the enlarger with
the lens wide open, and hold the negative perpendicular to the lens.
The dust is then side-lit and really shows up. It can be blown or
brushed off easily.)

I then make a test strip, a wide strip of paper placed in such a way
that it records all of the significant tones of the picture. If there are
people involved, I place the test strip so that I can see a face. Then I
make a guess as to the contrast filter and the time of exposure and
expose the whole strip. I long ago stopped using the step-system for
a few reasons. For one, by exposing the whole strip, I have become a
rather good guesser, for another, unless the picture is of an all-over
tone, the step-system doesn't help me at all because different areas
get different exposures in order to be the tones that I want. Lastly,
when I get a test that's fairly close to what I am after, it gives me a
great deal of information about the picture. Many times I can give
up on a negative at this point because it is clear that the picture is
not working out as a finished print. It could be about sharpness
or tonal or facial expression or just 'something about it' makes me
realize that it's not going to work out. I have just saved a lot of time
and paper. I need to always keep in mind that printing is interpretive. I rotate the test strips to different areas of the picture until
I get the density and contrast that I want overall. By now, I have
also identified areas where I want to dodge and burn, perhaps with
different filters, so that when I make the first full print I'm about
half-way there.

The first print gets fixed, rinsed, put up on the glass in the sink
and squeegeed off (one of my favorite activities). Then I sit and
look. At this point, I sometimes stop printing a picture because I

want to look at it for a week or so to decide if I want to make a
finished print or not, and, if yes, then how I want it to look. If I want
to continue, I will look at the print both right side up and upside
down to see where the eye goes and if it goes where I want it to.

This factor is a large determinant of dodging and burning as well as
a reconsideration of cropping decisions. Once I get a print right, I'll
make a few.
   Finally, a note about the light in the printing room. It should
be played with until it makes sense in terms of print 'dry-down.' I
prefer overall light in the room rather than a light over the fix tray
because it's easier on the eyes.

A photographer is walking in the park. She sees a bench. There are two couples on the bench. Each couple is very much in love. The two couples do not know each other. Just by coincidence, the situation is this:

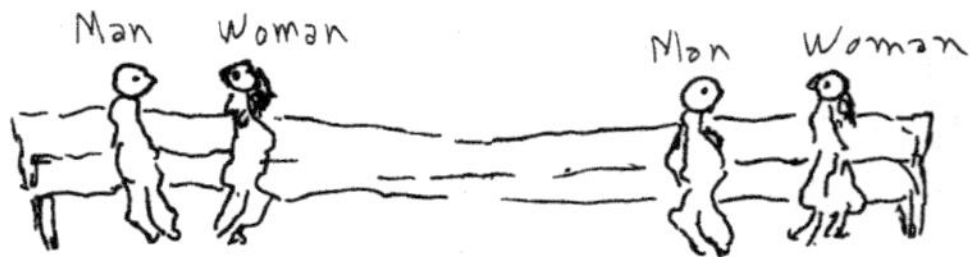

Both couples eyes are cast down and they are speaking of their love in shy, quiet tones. Their hands are folded on their laps. This, you must admit, is not an uncommon situation; it could be happening right now on a park bench somewhere.

Our photographer sees this, quietly goes over and makes a photograph like this:

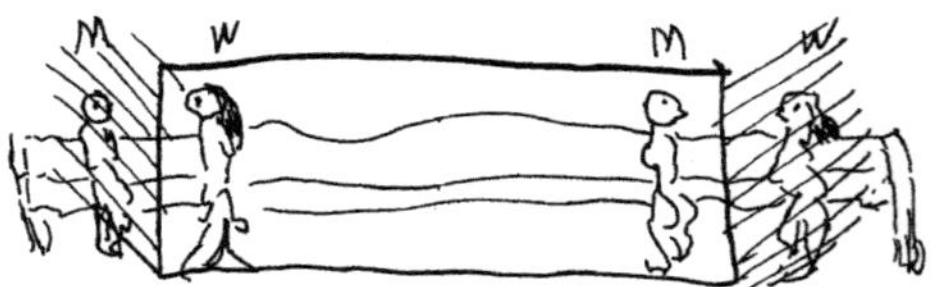

The picture is then hung in a gallery in an exhibition about how modern couples are having trouble relating to each other. No one will question it. An 'ologist' might even write a scholarly article addressing the issue.

Along comes the editor of *National Geographic* and he pushes the pyramids at Giza closer together so that they will fit the vertical format of his 'colonialist' magazine.

It's done with a computer rather than razor blades and rubber
cement. Everyone goes nuts about how you can no longer trust the
camera to tell the truth.

In 1888, Henry Peach Robinson was gluing and pasting as many
as 10 pictures together and re-photographing them and making
seamless Victorian melodrama. Photographs could never be
trusted on a factual level.

Art is a lie that reveals the truth. Pablo Picasso

Because the camera always frames what is in front of it, in a sense
everything photographed is 'out of context.' Since all photographs
slice time, they are also inherently 'out of context.' Even photographs that we call 'straight' are not 'true' for these two reasons
alone. All this before you even 'boot up.'

§§§§§

If one sees the function of photographic education as primarily
technical: learning optics, chemistry and the handling of machines,
the shift from chemical to digital methods will represent a major
upheaval.

On the other hand, if the aim of photography is to develop vision,
to find out what it is in me that corresponds to what I perceive as
phenomena, and to create a form in order to express that correspondence, then indeed the use of digital tools becomes a wonderful
expansion of possibilities.

As of now, the ability to scan negatives and edit lots of material
very fast is positive. Some of the prints being made are beautiful, a
kind of hybrid between a photographic print and a fine reproduc-
tion. Digital technology can help a person to 'range bigger' if their
artistic scope can handle it.

The fact that photographs can be more easily altered is a mixed blessing. The ease of doing this can make an artist go soft in the same way that electronics in music can seduce musicians to lose their edge.

The basic and most profound aspects of photographic education should remain the same. A person learns to deal with space, tone, color, perspective, time, choice of prospect, expression, relation to other people as subject, collaboration; not to mention history and aesthetics as well as the vast world of 'meaning' in the creation of photographs.

The shift to digital tools will not eliminate these aspects any more than the shift from film to video has changed the basic concepts of montage and narrative in motion pictures.

The ability to observe with rigor, to translate from three or four dimensions to two with real speed and clarity and to do it 'fresh' is still the central problem of learning photography and it doesn't really matter what the recording method is. This is an oversimplification.

New technologies have, and will continue to have, as profound an effect on the aesthetics of the medium as have the hand-held camera, modern color processing, fast films, electronic flash, etc. But I feel strongly that the underlying principles of making something that we think of as transcendent remain basically the same. It is like motion around a center core that is constant. I hope I'll still be able to get film and printing paper.

It's interesting to note that as this new technology develops and gets more accessible, there is a re-emergence in the use of 'historical' processes like platinum, palladium, carbro and cyanotype.

A great deal of the collage/montage work now being done on the computer has its aesthetic reference late 19th and early 20th century materials. Never before have so much gauze and so many peacock feathers loomed in galleries. Makes you think it's 1905 all over again.

Maybe time goes in two directions after all.

The following is a description of how I try to conduct a critique. I don't claim that it is either the correct or the 'best' way, but simply a system that has developed over the last 35 years or so and suits my thinking and spirit. It is quite effective in my classes.

For me, there are basically two ways to think about learning. The first considers a newborn to be a blank sheet (tabula rasa) or an empty vessel, and the process of learning is to 'acquire knowledge' through a series of experiences that we call 'education.' In other words, the sheet gets written on or the vessel gets filled. If the writing on the sheet is of high quality then the person has a 'good education.' Of course, the ability of each person to acquire knowledge varies a great deal depending on I.Q., desire and talent in different areas of study.

Another way to look at this issue is to think of a person as being born knowing everything – or that 'mind' is not so attached to an individual as we think – and that education is the process of assisting the person in becoming aware of what is already known on some subtle level. Perhaps this is why when we read or hear an idea or concept that is particularly profound, it always seem familiar and the thought 'of course' goes through our minds. So then the process of education becomes one of revealing or uncovering rather than that of acquiring.

The above can be seen as a terrible oversimplification of a very complex issue. However, the point of this theory is quite specific in terms of how I conduct a class, my assumption is that all of us have a direction to go in and we have to find that direction through the process of working in a medium, with intelligence, over a long period of time.

Style is the imprint of what one is on what one does.
René Daumal

If I accept this concept, then the only issue is how the class and
teacher can help a person to find and go in that direction.

First, we try to build the arena in which this can best take place.
A few rules and principles that are quite strict.
~ No rudeness
~ No competition
~ No telling the artist what the work means about them
  (a critique is not psychotherapy)
~ The class chooses what work will be talked about.
  (Students should feel free to ask that their work be dealt with
  because they need feedback.) No need to address every work in
  every class.

Here's the main principle:
The person whose work is being addressed can answer factual
questions in the beginning, i.e., where was the picture made, what
film, lens, etc. They can say nothing about intention, content, or
other meaning. At this time, the rest of the group can say anything
they like about the work, be it craft, aesthetics, politics, art history,
et al. They are free to say anything. They can report associations in
their minds, dreams and fantasies as long as it's about the work
and not about the person who made the work.

Something very interesting starts to take place if this is done with
openness and intelligence; the student is getting real information
about what their work is communicating to a group of people who
are being as honest and caring as possible. This information is for
the use of the student and they can do anything they want to with
it. The work never has to be defended, justified or explained. At this
point, if a student wants to talk about the work just discussed, they
can do so as much as they would like, and a long back and forth
discussion can take place.

The role of the teacher in this process is to moderate, and to be a participant along with everyone else.

The sole purpose of the critique is for students to gain insight about their work and have information that will help them to proceed toward the next stage of development. As a group works together from week to week, a level of trust and understanding can develop so that people are more willing to take chances both in the discussion, but more importantly, in their work. Then you've really done something worthwhile.

It is vitally important for the group, and especially the teacher, to make clear the difference between fact (a smaller aperture gives more depth of field) and opinion (this picture has a violent edge). Making this difference clear allows the discussion to range much bigger.

If I have something essential to communicate to another person, probably a good way to do this is to sit a reasonable distance from them and look straight at them as they look straight at me 'eye-to-eye.' If I am sitting on a lower seat than the other person, or if they other person is standing and I am sitting, then the relationship is altered in many ways both physically and psychologically.

§§§§§

In the 19th century, making a portrait was clearly a serious event. There were no 'snapshots' yet. Generally people dressed up (sometimes in ill-fitting, borrowed clothes), and, most importantly, the exposures were quite long, which in itself brought seriousness of expression more or less automatically. It is hardly possible to find a portrait done before 1900 that does not contain some quality of intensity and penetration.

The most ambitious portrait project between two people is probably the photographs that Alfred Stieglitz did with Georgia O'Keeffe. Stieglitz, on more than one occasion, referred to these pictures as a collaboration, rather than 'photographer and sitter.' It is clear in many of the pictures that O'Keeffe is bringing most of the energy to the event. A brilliant aspect of the Stieglitz-O'Keeffe pictures is how Stieglitz used exposure, development and printing style to express the emotional quality of the particular situation in which the picture was made. The prints range from high contrast graphic all the way over to the cusp of murky. Stieglitz was not a person to worry about style.

Some of the photographs are among the most erotically charged ever done, some are transcendent, and some are silly and melodramatic. Life on earth.

In the work of August Sander there is an aspect of portraiture that needs to be examined. Sander encouraged people to present themselves in ways that they felt best expressed who they were. Usually wearing the costume of their profession (identity), they then assumed the physical attitude of this self-image. Sander composed brilliantly and exercised impeccable craft in making these pictures.

All this leads to the threshold of what is important. In using this method, Sander manages (here's the mystery) to show us the role being played and, at the same time, the creature inside playing the role. In experiencing the humanity of another, I can sense my own humanity and my world expands in that moment.

Diane Arbus used Sander's method with some success in the 1950s and 60s. I don't think she ever reached the level of Sander because the work remained so much about herself. There is more to art than self-expression.

The current state of portraiture is that there is a barrel-full of smart, talented, aggressive people making a lot of loot describing the roles people take in clever ways. The newest thing seems to be getting physically closer than normal, which creates a feeling of discomfort (any feeling will do).

It's not a coincidence that some of the current leading portraitists are also fashion photographers who are really good at expressing surface in an appealing way. I'm stopping this before it becomes a rant.

A few how-to's:

When doing a portrait with a cut-film camera, there is preparation needed. Positioning the camera on the stand, framing, focusing, stopping down, inserting film, pulling slide, etc. All of this serves as a build-up to the moment of releasing the shutter. This has a profound effect on the emotional quality and intensity of the picture made.

With a small camera it is of course possible to capture a 'moment.'
There is more of a chance for the unexpected to occur. The trade off
is that with up to 36 chances it's easy for the whole thing to go soft
and lose any kind of formal or human tension.

If artificial light is needed and money is short, an excellent light
stand can be made with an empty gallon paint can, filled with
plaster of Paris, and a broomstick stuck in when it's wet. If a higher
stand is needed, duct tape can be used to add another broomstick.
   Hardware store clamp-on reflector lights with photoflood bulbs
give as good a light as the most expensive instruments. Foam-core
is pure white for color balance and is lightweight enough to tape
to things or hang from the ceiling with string; it provides instant
bounce for soft, but directional light. Different focal-length lenses
will describe physiognomy differently.

§§§§§

A strong portrait is also a strong photograph.

EXERCISE #8 SELF-PORTRAIT

There are several compelling reasons for a new photographer to
make some self-portraits.

First, it connects the photographer to the history of art in a real way
because there is a long tradition of self-portraiture in painting and
photography.

Secondly, it gets the person out from behind the camera. This
can start to open one up to the possibility of using the camera in
different ways as a light collecting device and not always an instru-
ment to look at things through.

If one of the central issues of learning the medium is to 'get interested' in a subject, then of course the self-portrait has that built in.
 Probably the most useful aspect of the self-portrait exercise is
that the photographer has to give up some amount of control (I
don't know what the picture will look like). This can introduce a
person to the idea of 'chance' as art-making.
 Editing moves to the prime position – where it belongs – and
better yet, if the metaphor sinks in, a whole world can open up for
the photographer. The entire concept of chance and luck is very
under-rated and under-used in European-American culture. I insist
on taking credit for everything good that happens and on blaming
others for everything bad.

All this from a self-portrait.

A Lakota woman named Elaine Jahner once wrote that what lies at the heart of the religion of hunting peoples is the notion that a spiritual landscape exists within the physical landscape. To put it another way, occasionally one sees something fleeting in the land, a moment when line, color, and movement intensify and something sacred is revealed, leading one to believe that there is another realm of reality corresponding to the physical one but different. Barry Lopez *Arctic Dreams*

In 1970, I moved from New York City to Warwick, New York. At that time, I had been photographing for about 14 years and was mostly involved in 'street photography.'

I began to photograph the landscape. I was concerned that it would be too easy. Some friends even suggested that I was 'copping out.' I learned a lot in the next few years.

In photographing nature you don't get the same kind of random events (gifts) that can make a 'street' photograph surprising and magic such as the turn of a head or a hat blowing off.

I began to realize that the content of street photography is often based on a kind of criticism or at least a sense of irony. The photographer is in a superior position to the subject as an observer who can isolate and shift context through choice of frame and timing of exposure.

Photographing people in public spaces also creates a level of tension and frequently a flow of adrenaline that is apparent in some of the photographs and contributes to the content.

The question becomes how to introduce emotional content in landscape photography without all the ammunition that one has in social situations.

Simple. Get a bigger camera. More detail, more control, plus the
seriousness of history. That should do it. Instantly you're hooked
onto O'Sullivan, Watkins, Weston, Adams, etc. 'Good company.' I'll
trade one tradition for another. But wait – let's look at Stieglitz and
Thelonious Monk and maybe at Kertész and certainly Balanchine. It
would be hard to find four more different artists. The 'thread' is that
no matter what the style or medium, their 'stamp' is unmistakable,
and it's not just the 'look.' It's deeper, much deeper. The image is
coming from within the artist, and the creative act is in correspondence with what we experience as physical reality.

Can I make a photograph of nature (the woods) that can be next
to one of my pictures of people on the street and it will sit there
with 'meaning?'

§§§§§

I give myself the advantage of using the same camera, lens and film
that I always use so that there is graphic continuity.

It must be said here that all of this thinking and explaining of my
processes is taking place 30 years later. When it was happening, I
was swimming in muddy water looking for something to grab onto.
The pictures precede the explanation.

I tried bigger cameras. I even dropped a borrowed 8x10 Deardorff
off its tripod on the ground and spent two weeks gluing, sanding
and refinishing.

It slowly began to dawn on me that you can't criticize nature
and that the kind of surprises one gets have to do with light, space,
texture, tone of air, and that a place is never the same twice. Luck is
sometimes about the shadow of a tree limb on a stone for a moment.

I was really starting to understand that a leaf floating on the
surface of a puddle with the light a certain way can be a significant
event.

55

I was beginning to see with the eyes of a child. Things were starting to lose their hierarchical nature. Everything was of equal value, and the 'content' was in the vision and craft.

One time, I was sitting looking out the window at the woods. It was twilight and my cat Goody, who was black, walked across my field of view. I realized something: there is no black in nature or rarely is. Dark is mysterious, black is not.

I started to make small prints on matte paper and to extend the tonal range as much as I could.

Ansel Adams is a pictorialist as much as any of the people that he railed against. He simply used a different visual system to create sentiment and idealization.

Dorothea Lange once said that the trouble with Ansel's pictures is that they were 'too photographic.' This is a telling statement if one accepts the concept and includes people like Harry Callahan and William Klein as well as a host of others as being 'too photographic.' Again we see that what might be called 'art' in photography is not in the print as physical object, but rather the art exists in that tiny yet infinite space between observation and recording. The thrill is in the balance, which can never be too precarious.

It's interesting to note here that it would be hard to imagine one saying that Van Gogh or De Kooning are 'too painterly.' Photography, once again, doesn't fold that easily into other visual media. I have not changed the subject. If, as a photographer, one looks at the history of landscape painting and then tries to 'hook on' with a camera, it becomes clear quite soon that the result will be rather flat both visually and emotionally. If one then tries to 'soup up' the prints for added drama, then the results can get really dumb. You can't improve nature.

What I can do if I'm interested is to go out and look for 'myself,' for a correspondence to the infinite variety of spaces, textures, light, air, movement, life and death, that is everywhere in the natural world.

He had drawn the curtains and was working by shaded light, like an acrobat in the semi-darkness of a circus, performing danger-ous new leaps in front of a gathering of experts before the public are let in. The precision, vigor and sureness of this kind of think-ing, which has not its equal anywhere in life, filled him with something like melancholy.

Robert Musil *The Man Without Qualities*

The very myth of the 'straight' photograph is one of the most misleading aspects in the history of the medium. There never was any such thing. It sets up camps and prevents us from understanding what we have as a medium and what we can do with it.

If one looks at pictures by Edward Weston and then goes to Point Lobos in California where he photographed for years, the extreme manipulations of camera work and printing that Weston practiced are clear in an instant. This doesn't mean that many of the photographs aren't wonderful, but he was manipulating the medium as much as any of the pictorialists that he was trying to kill off. It was a matter of style and vision, no more.

The difference between Ansel Adams and William Mortensen has nothing to do with 'purity' of vision or 'straightness.' It has to do with the use to which one puts the medium. Are black skies 'straighter' than soft focus?

§§§§§

We can certainly prefer the work of one photographer or group of photographers over another and even make arguments that one kind of work is better, more profound or more relevant to our lives than another. But it has nothing to do with 'straightness.'

We were speaking of the 'digital darkroom.' A bit of an oxymoron, but it's the term of the day. In pre-digital photography, a person chooses a set of tools and materials and then feels free to push as hard as possible on the limits of that particular medium. In other words, the very limitations create the arena for the struggle to take place. The expression of that struggle is a huge contributor to what we experience as expressive tension in viewing the work.

For example, I'm walking on the street and I see something marvelous happening right there on the sidewalk. I photograph it. When I develop the film and make a quick print I see that there is a car, shiny and bright right in the middle of the scene and it doesn't 'work' in the frame. Oh well, lost a good one; that's bad.

Cut to 'digital darkroom.' Remove car, fill in space with side-walk-street. It's seamless; no one can tell, not even me. That's good.

§§§§§

A fly fisherman died. He awoke to find himself in the most beautiful river he had ever seen. In his hand is the most perfect fishing rod imaginable, with a 'work-of-art' 16 Quill Gordon fly on the end of his line. He casts to a rising fish and hooks, lands and releases an exquisite 20-inch brown trout. 'I'm in heaven.'

He casts again with the same result. And again, and again, each time hooking and landing a perfect fish. Slowly it starts to occur to our fisherman that he may not be in heaven at all.

We live in an age where everything is
available but nothing is valuable.
E.L. Doctorow

I am not for a moment suggesting that new technologies should not be used, but used as tools rather than being automatically embraced just because they are the newest thing or because they make things easier or quicker.

One of the most unfortunate trends in photographic education is
the creation of a division between 'documentary' photography and
'fine art' photography.

All photographs describe and all photographs are expressive to
some degree because photographers make decisions in taking
pictures.

To draw lines and force students to take sides is poison.

§§§§§

Creating aesthetic ghettos makes it easy to avoid a discussion of
what constitutes 'quality' in art, which is, of course, the central
issue and the most difficult to address.

CONTENT – CONTEXT – INFLUENCE

I know that my photographs are influenced by photographers, painters, and writers of the past. They are also informed by my genetics, physical type, mental skills, perhaps even my astrological configuration. They are certainly affected by my upbringing, the culture of my youth and the culture of the present. They are affected by my economic status and my social relations, and by my psychological, spiritual, and aesthetic thrusts. My political point of view influences my work. Finally, the fact that all of these factors – as well as the many more that I am not aware of – are in constant flux makes it perfectly clear that I'll never figure the damn thing out. Nor do I want to. What I can do as an artist is to accept, and if possible even embrace the fact that the puzzle is infinite; to continue to work in a craft over a period of time and to assume that a true voice will emerge. The freedom that comes from this understanding is thrilling.

If I take off my shoe and use it to drive in a nail, what is the object in my hand?

If I take an old two-man saw and hang it on the wall of my office in the city, what is the object on the wall?

I recently found a spot at the Metropolitan Museum of Art in the African wing where you can stand and see nearly the whole history of European art of the 20th century. Without moving your feet, to your left is a perfect Picasso figure with the head tucked into the shoulder; straight ahead is a Brancusi painted by Paul Klee, to your right is a Leger, and so forth.

There is no question that artists are influenced and make use of the art that preceded them. We stand on the shoulders of those who came before. Robert Frank comes out of Bill Brandt and the filmmaker Jean Vigo, Diane Arbus out of August Sander. In

poetry Charles Olson from Ezra Pound. And in painting Richard
Diebenkorn was heavily influenced by Matisse and Edward Hopper
used Vermeer with pleasure. We take, we use, we even copy, we
try things, we write in the manner of (pastiche) in order to find our
voice – and we should.

Back to the Met. If I copy something and then present it in a different context (in a context that is completely different from the
intention of the maker and the culture of the maker) as did the
European artists with the African religious icons it is not the same
as "being influenced." It would be a kind of "post-modern" appro-
priation done with a hidden hand.

NOTE: *Duchamp, in moving the urinal to the plumbing shop to the
gallery and signing it R. Mutt addresses the issues of content and
context in a most direct and shocking manner. He also questions
if an artist must make the work at all – or can "recognition" be the
art itself.*

It would be quite simple to leave this discussions as a complaint
against the way European imperialism and white males in particular took things made for spiritual communication or the preserva-
tion of esoteric knowledge and turned them into egocentric fame
and money-making objects.

The logical conclusion of such an argument is that the world
would be better off if everything had just stayed where it was and
there had been no communication between cultures at all. That's
not how things work. The whole business is far more complex and
interesting than that.

When I was leaving my full-time teaching job last fall, I was speaking with John Levine on the telephone. John is a psychiatrist, who teaches at Harvard Medical School. He was in the first photography class I taught and became interested in the relationship between photographic, musical and emotional tone.

I told John I had a strange feeling; although 65 and retiring, part of me still doesn't know 'what I want to be when I grow up.' 'That's neoteny,' John said. He went on to explain that neoteny is a biological term which is used metaphorically to describe adults who, while functioning at a mature level, retain and utilize traits from earlier stages of development: curiosity; imagination; playfulness; a zest for learning new things; and a connection with childhood feelings and fantasies. Many older artists are in that situation, he said. 'It's a positive adaptation. It's also part of how they got to be artists in the first place.'

§§§§§

I send a prayer of gratitude for the experience of standing in awe at the sight of birds flying past a bare tree against the winter sky.

Œpress is a small press establishing a publication list of unique titles and authors with a signed first run limited edition printing of 300 copies.

§§§§§

RIT Cary Graphic Arts Press is the publication arm of the Melbert B. Cary, Jr. Graphic Arts Collection at Rochester Institute of Technology.

§§§§§

Philip Perkis

Began photography in the U.S. Air Force in 1957 while serving as B36 tail-gunner. ¶ Attended San Francisco Art Institute, studied with Ansel Adams, Dorothea Lange, and John Collier Jr. ¶ Came to New York in 1962. ¶He has taught at many schools and offered numerous workshops around the world. ¶ Served as Chair of Photography, Pratt Institute. ¶ Currently on graduate faculty, School of Visual Arts, and Tisch, NYU. ¶ Guggenheim Fellow, NEA and CAPS grants. *Warwick Mountain Series,* Nexus Press. ¶ Numerous solo and group exhibitions. ¶ Work is represented in many museum collections. ¶ Monograph, *The Sadness of Men* (in process).

§§§§§

This title was set in Georgia 9.5/12.7. Production by Marnie Soom, Amelia Hugill-Fontanel, D. Michael Hansen, Diana Mross. Printed by Lulu.com.